Chapters of Age

Peter Riley

Open House Editions

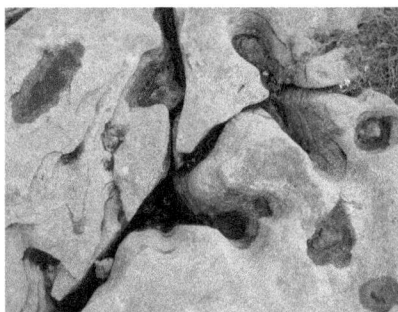

Published by Open House Editions
an imprint of Leafe Press
www.leafepress.com

Cover photography by Beryl Riley

ISBN 978-0-9574048-0-9

Chapters of Age

Stone landscapes of Inishmore and Burren, May 2010

Chapters of age: increasing anxiety,
Histories beyond credence,
Massive stone forts in mist.

Ruins of small monastic settlements.
Dull pain to right of middle back.
Stone distances beyond thought.

Use of walking stick to lessen this pain,
Inclined to the side of the road.
Singing and laughter from stone heaps.

Loss of secure equilibrium in darkness
With tension headache.
The massive lintel.

●

In Carna they sang as nowhere else
And I did sing, at least once I did.
Nobody held my hand.

"I kissed my love by the factory wall"
Did I?
Liability to mental paralysis when challenged.

And sing still and louder sing,
Psalmic impulsions rolling over the moor
Seeking an imperfect cadence.

●

A man lives in a kind of box in the garden.
Where is the musician or architect
Who built me this weary smile?

The blue and white teacloth,
Symbol of a domestic contract. Outside,
All the world is grey.

This worry in the evening
That the young of earth might wreck everything,
But all they do is fall over

Singing "Dirty old town". Outside
The windows and five fields further on
The stone tractates become statutory.

●

Thatched cottage capitulating to damp,
The chair outside the door
Where he used to sit

Facing south across the chevaux-de-frise
Remembering blood on snow, Lord,
Keep us from mystery and impotent rage.

Saw everything from there, the rich
And the poor, the cloud descending,
The cattle driven over the cliff.

●

Thousands of gentians (spring, 5-petal)
And mountain avens
In the cracks of limestone pavements.

A line between shadow and light
Full of bone and flint
Full of flint and bone.

Lines across the earth, head
Looks at foot, foot steps across
Gaps in stone where gentians grow.

God I used to have such a pure foot
You couldn't see a single vein on it.
How our forms rush to the gate.

How matter obstruct us
And yet forms
The delicate street at night

And the endless stone deserts
At which the heart grows weary
And the mind smoulders.

•

Bleak godforsaken peninsula becomes
Bleak godforsaken transport development.
Earthly tides, come and go.

A quarter mile walk to a locked gents.
The coast too is all rock and gap
And here comes the inspector hopping.

"What are all those fuzzy looking things out there?"
Trees, clouds, stones, floaters,
Little bright-eyes calling me.

•

These lonely towers falling to ruin.
The rook flies straight in the window
Causing eructations.

Law school in a stone ring "Old age is either
Wholly centralised or the centre atrophies."
Centrifugal dehydration mechanism.

Megalithic tombs surmounting the thin fields
That run off into the distance harbouring
Old men who ran away with babies.

"Over a thousand years later a newly-born baby
Was buried in front of the portal".
Loss of short-term memory.

Finding the way to the bathroom
In the middle of the night half asleep
Strange shadow, shed door ajar again.

•

Baby curled up very small in the centre.
Two men doing a fiddle combat.
Unbearable histories,

Famine and persecution,
Fighters disguised as priests or violinists
On the night path over the hill

With nothing said, only the wind in the hazel bushes
That are eating up the open land, tossing
Back and forth over the graves of heroes

Who died for a free Ireland
Now
Mortgaged to international finance,

That secret chapel in the woods
And the wide routes thereto across the open pastures
And poor little Jimmy Murphy under the deep green mossy bank.

●

And many another, as plentiful as the stars
And the stones underfoot, of which at least two will be raised
And carefully placed at the limits of our science.

Dig my grave both wide and deep, a marble stone
At my head and feet, and to my chest there comes
A turtle dove, to tell the world I died for love.

Tell me something else, tell me the source and extent
Of this silence, not in the grave but in the homes and
Parliaments of the world, heart of stone.

"This awful silence that emanates from me, standing there
Trying to remember what real people would say
In the circumstances" head stone foot stone cumulus.

Head stone foot stone cumulus, the day
Is ended and lost, nobody said anything to relieve misfortune
The day is destroyed.

Unbaptised children set in separate graveyards
Mere bits of walled-off moor with neither head nor
Foot stones but massive cumulus.

Head guides foot the route home.
All I asked was a legal answer,
A ring under cumulus.

·

What then is the lesson of the stone tractates, what
Is the tune they sing back to us after all our naming?
"A Labouring Man" and his fear.

The questions flying at us every day —
What is the plant with dark green leaves and
Tiny white flowers? What is the answer to fear?

For there are answers to fear,
Common or garden,
That singing up the coast.

Explanatory notes:

"Nobody held my hand". In the social singing of ornamental song in Irish, for which Carna in Connemara was specially well known, it was the custom to give the singer support through the difficult performance by holding his or her hands during the song.

"chevaux de frise" (Fresian horses). In this case, big elongated stones set in the ground in a mass in front of the fort, to hinder invasion on horseback.

"The cattle driven over the cliff". This took place on Inishmore in 1881 as part of a protest against evictions and land-grabbing.

Entire sentences are quoted from:

W.B. Yeats, Tarjei Vesaas, (*The Birds* and T*he Boat in the Evening*), William Carlos Williams, Georg Simmel, the on-site information board at Poulnabrone, and verses of three British songs, one of which I didn't know was by Ewan MacColl -- I heard it performed by a semi-derelict trio in a hotel bar in Clonakilty.

Peter Riley, 2012